LAST NIGHT'S READING

ILLUSTRATED ENCOUNTERS *with* EXTRAORDINARY AUTHORS

KATE GAVINO

PENGUIN BOOKS

PENGUIN BOOKS
An imprint of Penguin Random House LLC
375 Hudson Street
New York, New York 10014
penguin.com

Some of the selections appeared on the *Last Night's Reading* blog on Tumblr.

ISBN 978-0-14-312731-4

Printed in the United States of America

1   3   5   7   9   10   8   6   4   2

Designed by Alissa Rose Theodor

TABLE OF CONTENTS

AUTHORS AREN'T
KNOWN AS THE MOST
ATTRACTIVE
BUNCH...

HENRIK IBSEN
1828 ~ 1906

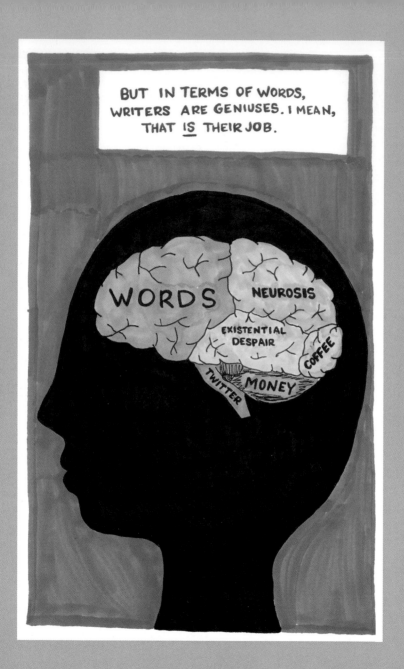

THEY CAN WRITE A SINGLE SENTENCE THAT SLAYS YOU WITH ITS TRUTH . . .

WRITING IS A SOLITARY ACTIVITY, BUT AT A READING, WRITERS ARE WITH THEIR AUDIENCE, TALKING ABOUT WHAT MATTERS MOST TO THEM.

AND I GET TO SHARE WHAT I SEE AND HEAR WITH YOU.

KNOWLEDGE

"I WRITE EMOTIONAL ALGEBRA."
—ANAÏS NIN

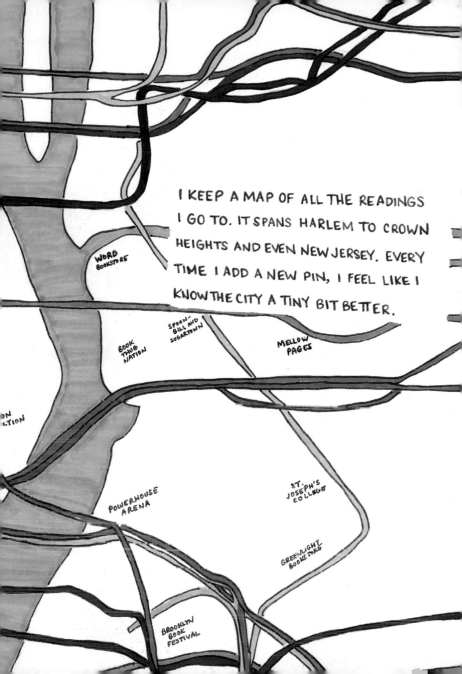

I KEEP A MAP OF ALL THE READINGS I GO TO. IT SPANS HARLEM TO CROWN HEIGHTS AND EVEN NEW JERSEY. EVERY TIME I ADD A NEW PIN, I FEEL LIKE I KNOW THE CITY A TINY BIT BETTER.

DOUBT
IS MY
NATIVE
LAND,
WHERE I CAN
STAND
WITHOUT THE
SHACKLES
of
CERTAINTY.

—LESLIE JAMISON
11/15/14

BEAUTY LIES **NOT** IN THE QUICK REACTION OR THE DECISIVE MOVE BUT IN THE CONTEMPLATION OF POSSIBILITY.

—LORRIE MOORE
10/25/13

my OVERARCHING
AIM IS TO
SIMPLY

MAKE SENSE.

—CHARLES D'AMBROSIO
11/15/14

To be a good **OPTIMIST**, you have to be a good **CYNIC**, too... **INTELLIGENT** OPTIMISM IS ABLE TO BEAT CYNICISM AT ITS OWN GAME.

—COLUM McCANN
11/9/13

THERE'S A
DIFFERENCE
BETWEEN THE
LITERAL TRUTH
AND THE
EMOTIONAL TRUTH.

—MARY GAITSKILL
10/23/14

THERE ARE
MORE TRUTHS
in FICTION
THAN REALITY.

—WALTER
MOSLEY
9/30/14

NO THEORETICAL
MODEL CAN ENCOMPASS
the COMPLEXITY

OF WHAT IT MEANS TO BE

HUMAN.

—SIRI HUSTVEDT
3/18/14

DON'T EXPLAIN
IT TO DEATH—
OR IT CEASES
TO BE

MAGIC.

—LEV GROSSMAN
3/17/14

IT'S OUR JOB
TO TAKE
ENTROPY
and
RANDOMNESS
AND FIND
MEANING...

—KHALED HOSSEINI
6/6/14

Do

WRITE WHAT
YOU KNOW...

IF

WHAT YOU
KNOW IS
INTERESTING.

—SALMAN
RUSHDIE
8/25/14

WE DON'T USE OUR BRAINS. WE ARE OUR BRAINS.

—STEVEN PINKER
5/29/14

WE READ
BOOKS TO
REHEARSE
for LIFE.

—LOIS LOWRY
10/19/14

THERE'S A LOT
TO BE SAID FOR
AMATEURS...
IGNORANCE CAN
PLAY AN IMPORTANT
PART IN ENCOURAGING
US TO
LOOK
HARDER.

—GEOFF DYER
11/26/13

·LOVE·

"BEAUTY IS WHATEVER GIVES JOY."
—EDNA ST. VINCENT MILLAY

MY VERY FIRST LITERARY EVENT IN NEW YORK WAS THE BROOKLYN BOOK FESTIVAL. I COULDN'T BELIEVE SO MANY AUTHORS WERE IN ONE PLACE FOR FREE. AT THE END OF THE DAY I WAS BOTH EXHAUSTED AND INSPIRED, A COMBINATION OF FEELINGS I NOW CAN'T HELP BUT EQUATE WITH LOVE.

THERE IS
NO WRONG
WAY TO FIND
SOMETHING
YOU LOVE.

—NEIL GAIMAN
10/31/14

LOVE
and ROMANCE
ARE HARDLY
THE SAME THING...
LOVE CANNOT
BE REDUCED TO
ROMANCE.

—TIPHANIE YANIQUE
11/21/14

A BOOK
IS A VERY
DEMANDING

LOVE
LETTER

TO
SOMEONE.

-GARY SHTEYNGART
4/17/14

THE WORLD WILL WHITTLE YOU DOWN ENOUGH— A MOTHER NEVER SHOULD.

—MEG WOLITZER
6/7/14

LOVE ISN'T A THING, AFTER ALL, BUT AN ENDLESS SERIES OF SINGLE ACTS.

—RICHARD FORD
2/21/15

I DON'T WANT
TO LIVE IN A WORLD
WHERE I HAVE TO
APOLOGIZE
FOR LIKING
WHAT I LIKE.

—CHIMAMANDA NGOZI
ADICHIE 3/19/14

THE LEAST LIKELY
CHARACTERS IN
OUR LIVES ARE
USUALLY THE SOURCES
of GRACE.

—RICK MOODY
11/18/14

I AM
WORTHY
—and—
DESERVING
of the
SPACE
THAT I
OCCUPY.

—JANET MOCK
10/22/14

THE WORLD IS A PLACE OF FEELING... TRY TO TAKE POSSESSION OF THAT EXPERIENCE.

—DONALD ANTRIM
9/24/15

A PIECE of ART
CAN SOMETIMES
unlock
YOU IN A WAY
NOTHING ELSE HAS
MANAGED TO SO FAR.
    —RAINBOW ROWELL
      5/29/14

GIVE YOURSELF
OVER TO YOUR WORK
and THE HUMANITY
WILL RESONATE.

— TAVI GEVINSON
10/22/14

·FUN·

"LIFE IS SOMETIMES SAD AND OFTEN DULL,
BUT THERE ARE CURRANTS IN THE CAKE."
−NANCY MITFORD

SAPPHIRE
8/23/14

CHIMAMANDA
NGOZI ADICHIE
3/19/14

AS A CONSTANT DOODLER, I FIND MYSELF DRAWING AUTHORS' SHOES QUITE OFTEN. AMIDST THE SEA OF SENSIBLE LOAFERS AND FLATS, THERE ARE A FEW STANDOUTS, AND I HAVE COMMITTED THEM TO MEMORY.

IF YOU'RE NOT
ENJOYING SOMETHING,
IT'S ALMOST
always
BECAUSE YOU'RE
DOING IT TOO
fast.

—DONNA TARTT
10/29/13

GET
more
CONFUSED.

–GEORGE
SAUNDERS
10/5/13

TAKE THE
FAMILIAR
and
MAKE IT
STRANGE.
—LYDIA DAVIS
4/2/14

I READ IN A CHILDISH WAY AND GET SWEPT AWAY TO SUCH A DEGREE THAT I LACK THE WHEREWITHAL TO ASK WHETHER IT'S GOOD or BAD.

—JENNIFER EGAN
11/6/14

DISCERNMENT CAN BE THE *ENEMY* of PLEASURE.

—ROSIE SCHAAP
5/15/14

WORST ADVICE
I'VE EVER GOTTEN:
GO
OUTSIDE
— and —
PLAY.

-R.L. STINE
7/9/14

FUNNY

ALWAYS
HELPS
OUT THE
SCARY.

-KELLY
LINK
2/5/15

COMEDY LIVES IN UNCOMFORTABLE PLACES.

—MINDY KALING
10/11/14

LAUGHTER
IS SO
ABSTRACT
THAT IT IS THE
HIGHEST
POINT
of
UNDERSTANDING
SOMEONE.
—MARJANE SATRAPI
10/17/14

HUMOR IS *always* DEPLOYED AS A STRATEGY.

—BILLY COLLINS
10/28/14

·CREATIVITY·

"YOU DON'T MAKE GOOD ART OUT of GOOD INTENTIONS."
—GUSTAVE FLAUBERT

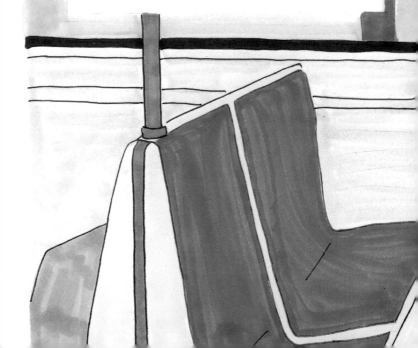

AFTER A PARTICULARLY STIRRING READING, I GET LOST IN WHAT I LIKE TO CALL "THE CLOUD." THE AUTHOR'S WORDS ARE STILL BUZZING AROUND IN MY MIND, AND I HAVE THE ALL-CONSUMING URGE TO CREATE SOMETHING. I KNOW I'M ESPECIALLY INSPIRED WHEN I MISS MY SUBWAY STOP.

WE ALL WANT A
PERFECT WORK OF
ART, BUT I'M NOT
UNHAPPY WITH A
FLAWED ONE, WHERE
YOU CAN SEE WHAT THE
ARTIST WAS TRYING FOR.
—MICHAEL
CUNNINGHAM
5/10/14

A WRITER IS
SOMEONE WHO
FINDS IT HARD
TO WRITE.

— E.L. DOCTOROW
5/29/14

I WAKE UP IN
A SWEAT OVER
ADJECTIVES

—CARL HIAASEN
5/31/14

BE RUTHLESS. THROW OUT WHOLE CHUNKS. MAKE FALSE STARTS. EVERYTHING WILL STAY ALIVE IN YOUR MEMORY.

—ANNE RICE
7/13/14

WE NEED
ART
and
BEAUTY
BECAUSE
SURVIVAL
is
INSUFFICIENT.

—EMILY ST. JOHN MANDEL
9/8/14

CELEBRATE
COMPLETION
NOT
PUBLICATION.

—AMY HEMPEL
10/30/14

IF YOU CAN
THINK IT,
SOMEONE IS
PROBABLY
WORKING ON IT
RIGHT NOW...
IT IS BOTH
EXHILARATING
and
TERRIFYING.
—MARGARET ATWOOD
12/3/14

BEING AN ARTIST IS SCARY. WHEN WE SAY A LINE LIKE IT'S OUR LAST BREATH OR JUMP IN THE AIR LIKE WE'RE TRYING TO REACH JUPITER, WE REALLY MEAN IT.

—NTOZAKE SHANGE
10/15/14

PART of BEING A
POET
IS BEING A
FAILED
MUSICIAN.
—MEGHAN O'ROURKE
11/11/14

I HAVE SPENT MY
WHOLE LIFE LOOKING
FOR THINGS THAT
EXIST ONLY FOR ME.
WE ARE CREATORS,
AND THAT IS OUR
BURDEN.

— TAIYE SELASI
11/20/14

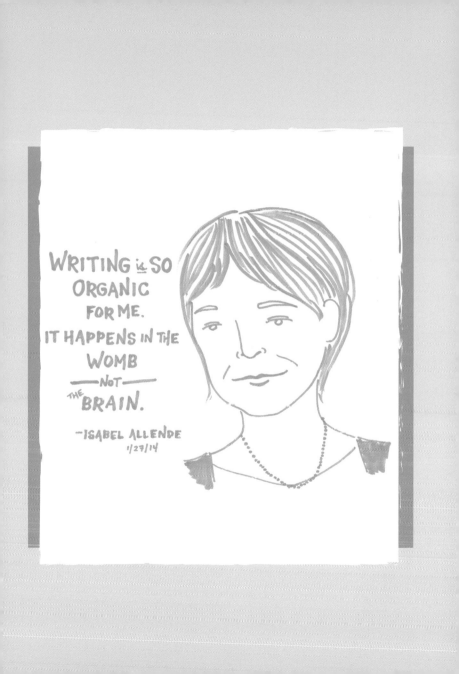

WRITING is SO
ORGANIC
FOR ME.
IT HAPPENS IN THE
WOMB
— NOT —
THE BRAIN.

—ISABEL ALLENDE
1/27/14

THERE HAS TO
BE A REASON
FOR EVERYTHING
YOU DO —
OTHERWISE
IT'S JUST A
GIMMICK.

—CHIP KIDD
10/14/13

·STORYTELLING·

"LET YOUR FICTION GROW OUT of THE LAND BENEATH YOUR FEET."
—WILLA CATHER

A MARK OF A GOOD STORYTELLER IS THE ABILITY TO COME UP WITH ELOQUENT, MEANINGFUL CONVERSATION ON THE SPOT. ONCE, AT AN AWARD CEREMONY, TONI MORRISON RUSHED PAST ME, AND I SAID...

THERE IS
SO MUCH IN
LIFE
STRAIGHT-
FORWARD
LANGUAGE
IS UNEQUAL To.

—EIMEAR McBRIDE
11/1/14

THE _only_ WAY TO
ARRIVE AT THE
END of A STORY
IS THROUGH
GROPING in THE DARK.
-PAUL THEROUX
10/12/14

IN ORDER TO
BE FREE...
WRITE VERY
QUICKLY *and*
GET RID
of THE NOTION *of*
QUALITY.

—KARL OVE KNAUSGAARD
6/4/14

EVERY STORY
IS SPUN FROM
SOMEONE
ELSE'S STORY.

—HELEN OYEYEMI
3/7/14

WE TELL STORIES
BECAUSE IT'S
IN OUR D<u>N</u>A. THAT
GAP BETWEEN
^{THE} READER
and
^{THE} STORY
IS WHERE MAGIC
TAKES PLACE.

—LAURIE HALSE
ANDERSON
3/24/14

A **SMALL** STORY TELLS *the* **BIG** STORY EVERY TIME.

—JAMES McBRIDE
6/7/14

THE MEANING OF A STORY IS NOT A STATIC THING YOU HAVE TO "GET." IT OCCURS WHEN A DISTANCE HAS BEEN Traversed.
—JONATHAN FRANZEN
4/2/14

WHEN YOU HAVE NO CHOICE, WHEN IT HAUNTS YOU... THAT'S THE TIME YOU TELL YOUR STORY.

—EDWIDGE DANTICAT
1/10/14

THE ABSOLUTE SAFETY of YOUR SOUL WILL DEPEND ON WHETHER YOU CAN FIND THE COMMUNITY OR THE COURAGE TO BEAR WITNESS TO WHAT HAS HAPPENED TO YOU.

—JUNOT DÍAZ
9/3/13

SET OUT TO
TELL
STORIES,
THEN
ACCIDENTALLY
WRITE A
NOVEL...

—KRISTOPHER
JANSMA
8/2/14

WORDS ARE OFTEN <u>NOT</u> ENOUGH, BUT A GREATER DANGER IS TO LET A SEPULCHRAL SOLEMNITY DESCEND UPON <u>YOU</u>.

—MARTIN AMIS
12/8/14

SOMETIMES
YOU HAVE TO
DISGUISE
the
ORDINARY
TO WRITE
MORE
TRUTHFULLY.
-NELL FREUDENBERGER
11/6/14

·STRENGTH·

"I PROTEST ANY ABSOLUTE CONCLUSION."
—GEORGE ELIOT

I'VE ENCOUNTERED THE SAME
SEEING EYE DOG AT MULTIPLE
READINGS THROUGHOUT THE CITY.
HE ALWAYS SITS PERFECTLY STILL
THE WHOLE TIME, LOOKING CONTENT
AND AT PEACE WITH THE WORLD.

MAYBE OUR
GIFT
IS OUR
ABILITY TO
PERSIST.

—CHANG-RAE LEE
1/7/14

Home IS NOT A COUNTRY, ESPECIALLY WHEN the COUNTRY HAS NEVER LEARNED TO BE AT HOME WITH ITS PAST.

—RITA DOVE

3/12/15

MY JOB IS
TO COACH
MYSELF
TO A PLACE
WHERE I WILL
WILLINGLY
N<u>O</u>T GO.

- CHUCK PALAHNIUK
4/11/14

I HIGHLY
RECOMMEND
FAILURE
AS A FORM OF
INSPIRATION.

—JULIE OTSUKA
9/21/14

THERE IS ALWAYS **HO<u>PE</u>**,

BUT ONLY IF THAT HOPE IS TURNED INTO **AC<u>TIO</u>N**.

-DAVID MITCHELL
5/31/14

BLOW UP
the
MACHINE
from the
INSIDE.

—ELISSA SCHAPPELL
9/21/14

CONSTRAINTS
CAN
UNWITTINGLY
OPEN
SO MANY
DOORS.
—LINDSAY HUNTER
11/9/14

MY WORK
WOULD NOT
EXIST WITHOUT
THE ENVY
THAT, IN TIME,
BECOMES
GRATITUDE.

—LOUISE GLÜCK
11/19/14

PAIN
IS A
TOUCHSTONE,

A TEACHER THAT WILL
BETTER ENABLE
US TO

EMBRACE
ITS
OPPOSITE.

—TRACY K. SMITH
3/11/14

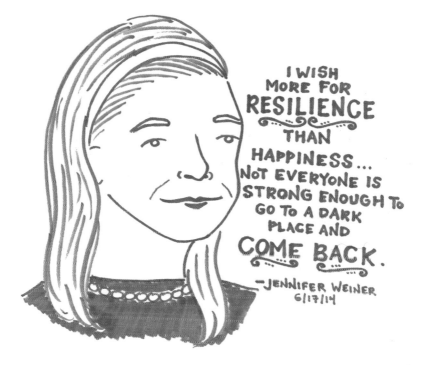

I WISH MORE FOR **RESILIENCE** THAN HAPPINESS... NOT EVERYONE IS STRONG ENOUGH TO GO TO A DARK PLACE AND **COME BACK.**

—JENNIFER WEINER
6/17/14

NOTICE HOW DURING AN AVALANCHE, THERE'S SOMETHING REAL THAT PERSISTS AND ⇒SHINES⇐ THROUGH THE RUBBLE...

—SHEILA HETI
12/12/13

IT'S OUR JOB TO SEE THE **PERSON** IN FRONT of US, AND IF THAT MEANS HAVING AN <u>UNCOMFORTABLE</u> <u>CONVERSATION</u>, HAVE THAT CONVERSATION. <u>PLEASE</u>.

—CLAUDIA RANKINE
11/13/14

THE WHITE, CRITICAL GAZE DISTORTS YOUR BEING, — BUT — IF YOU WRITE AWAY FROM IT OR REGARDLESS OF IT, THE WORLD IS YOURS.

—Toni Morrison
12/10/14

To WRITE
IS TO BE
IN DIALOGUE
WITH YOUR
PAIN.

—DANI SHAPIRO
2/18/14

Luck IS MERELY THE **TEMPORARY** **STATE** of OUTRUNNING **YOUR** **IMPENDING** **DISASTERS.**

—COLSON WHITEHEAD
3/11/15

·IDENTITY·

"WHEN I DISCOVER WHO I AM, I'LL BE FREE."
—RALPH ELLISON

I ONCE SAT NEAR JOAN DIDION AT A READING.
I HAVE A SOFT SPOT FOR EVENTS THAT DRAW
TINY AUDIENCES. AT THOSE GATHERINGS,
MORE THAN EVER, YOU GET THE SENSE
OF BEING A READER SUPPORTING AN AUTHOR
YOU LOVE — PROBABLY THE ONLY THING
JOAN DIDION AND I HAVE IN COMMON.

ONLY *you* KNOW HOW *you* FEEL.

—ANN PATCHETT
12/10/13

I LOVE BEING A
PART of THE HUMAN
RACE BUT I ALSO
LIKE to STAND
APART and SAY,
"BY THE WAY, YOU ALL
ARE DISGUSTING."
—JAMAICA KINCAID
4/3/14

EVERY "ISM" SHOULD CONSIDER the MULTIPLICITIES of IDENTITY.

—ROXANE GAY
9/21/14

IT'S NECESSARY TO UNDERSTAND THE WORKINGS of THE WORLD, BUT MORE NECESSARY TO UNDERSTAND THE WORKINGS of YOUR OWN PERSPECTIVE.

—JONATHAN SAFRAN FOER
3/13/14

THE **DEEPER** WE
GO INTO A CHARACTER,
THE **DARKER** AND MORE
MYSTERIOUS IT GETS...
WE ARE ALL
UNKNOWABLE.
—ANDRE DUBUS III
11/21/14

EVERY DAISY IN EVERY FIELD HAS AN IDENTITY THAT'S JUST AS STRONG AS YOUR OWN. IF YOU TRULY ACCEPT THAT, IT CANNOT HELP BUT CHANGE YOUR LIFE.

— TOM ROBBINS
5/27/14

WE WRITE
TO
INFORM
OURSELVES
OF
OURSELVES.

—JULIA FIERRO
7/15/14

AMERICA
IS STRANGE
IN ALL THE
WAYS THAT
IT ISN'T
SURPRISING.

—TEJU COLE
4/13/14

YOU WRITE
AS YOU ARE...
WHO YOU ARE
SEEPS OUT

THROUGH THE
HOLES in THE
LETTERS.

–AMY BLOOM
8/15/14

WE ARE *always* BE<u>COMING</u>. IT *never* STOPS.

—RICHARD BLANCO
10/2/14

GENRE
— AND —
GENDER
HAVE THAT
IN COMMON:
THEY'RE BOTH
MARKETING
TERMS

—KATE ZAMBRENO
7/1/14

THE NOTION of A
FIXED IDENTITY
SEEMS AT ODDS
WITH WHAT IT FEELS
LIKE TO BE
ALIVE...

—JEFFREY EUGENIDES
4/9/14

IT'S REMARKABLE
THAT IN THIS DAY
and AGE, AN UNLIKABLE
WOMAN IS NASTY and
AWFUL, AND AN
UNLIKABLE MAN
IS AN

ANTI-HERO.

—GILLIAN
FLYNN
4/24/14

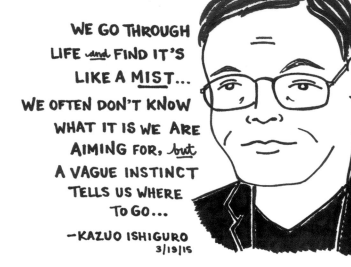

WE GO THROUGH
LIFE and FIND IT'S
LIKE A MIST...
WE OFTEN DON'T KNOW
WHAT IT IS WE ARE
AIMING FOR, but
A VAGUE INSTINCT
TELLS US WHERE
TO GO...

—KAZUO ISHIGURO
3/19/15

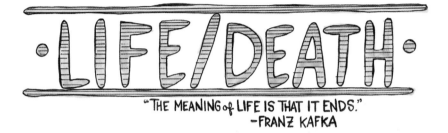

LIFE/DEATH

"THE MEANING of LIFE IS THAT IT ENDS."
—FRANZ KAFKA

MY FAVORITE READING TOOK PLACE IN THE CATACOMBS OF GREEN-WOOD CEMETERY. FEW THINGS MAKE YOU A BETTER LISTENER THAN BEING SURROUNDED BY THE DEAD.

A GOOD VILLAIN IS HARD TO REPLACE, BUT AS I SAY: ALL MEN MUST DIE.

—GEORGE R.R. MARTIN
10/26/14

THE MEANING of LIFE
THAT I'VE COME
AROUND TO IS
CONNECTION
and
AWARENESS...

— JOHN GREEN
5/31/14

MAYBE the TRUTH
of GETTING OLDER IS
THAT THERE ARE
LESS and LESS THINGS
To MAKE FUN of, UNTIL
THERE'S NOTHING
YOU'RE SURE YOU'LL
NEVER BE.

—JENNY OFFILL
11/1/14

IT WOULD BE EASY TO BELIEVE IN GOD IF WE KNEW HE EXISTED— BUT IT WOULDN'T BE MUCH *fun.*

— NICOLE KRAUSS
6/4/14

I NEED
LOSS
BEFORE
I CAN
BEGIN.

-COLM TÓIBÍN
10|20|14

I HAVE VERY
LITTLE FEAR OF
GETTING OLDER,
BUT I LIVE IN CONSTANT
DREAD THAT AN
EVIL GENIE WILL MAKE
ME RELIVE MY
TWENTIES.

-ELIZABETH GILBERT
6/24/14

WHEN I DIE,
TAKE MY BODY
TO AN
ICE CREAMATORIUM

THEN I'D LIKE A
TRADITIONAL
Sundae Service.

-DAVID SEDARIS
6/3/14

OUR LIVES ARE
FRAMED BY TWO
DARKNESSES WE
DON'T UNDERSTAND:
THE DARKNESS
BEFORE BIRTH
and
THE DARKNESS
AFTER DEATH.

—ALICE McDERMOTT
10/9/14

NO NOSTALGIA
HURTS AS MUCH
AS NOSTALGIA
~~for~~ THINGS THAT
NEVER EXISTED.

-RABIH ALAMEDDINE
1/7/15

THE NAME OF
OUR BEAUTIFUL
REWARD IS NOT
PROFIT.
ITS NAME IS
FREEDOM.

—URSULA K. LEGUIN
11/19/14

A HAPPY ENDING is
A MATTER of WHEN
THEY ROLL THE CREDITS.

—WILLIAM GIBSON
11/12/13

LASTNIGHTSREADING.com